# "Echoes of Earth: Stories of Resilience and Renewal in the Face of Climate Change"

Nadir Hussain Hazarika

# Preface

In a world where the impacts of climate change grow more pronounced with each passing day, the resilience of humanity and the natural world offers a beacon of hope. "Echoes of Earth: Stories of Resilience and Renewal in the Face of Climate Change" is a collection born from this spirit of endurance and adaptation.

Within these pages, you'll find stories that traverse the globe, exploring the diverse ways in which individuals and communities confront and overcome the challenges posed by a changing climate. From innovative solutions and ancient wisdom to acts of bravery and moments of introspection, these tales highlight the indomitable spirit that drives us to protect our planet and each other.

As you delve into this collection, may you be inspired by the courage, creativity, and resilience of those who, in the face of adversity, choose to echo the Earth's call for renewal. It is our hope that these stories will not only entertain but also motivate you to join the collective effort in forging a sustainable future.

Thank you for embarking on this journey with us.

Warm regards,
Nadir Hussain Hazarika

# Table of Contents:

# Part 1: The Awakening

The small coastal town of Seaview Cove was a place where the rhythm of the ocean dictated the pace of life. Its sandy shores were lined with colorful beach houses, and the salty breeze carried the laughter of children playing in the surf. But beneath the idyllic facade, a silent crisis loomed, one that threatened to disrupt the delicate balance of life by the sea.

Lila Bennett was a young marine biologist who had grown up in Seaview Cove, her childhood filled with memories of exploring tide pools and watching dolphins dance in the waves. But as she returned to her hometown after years of studying marine biology abroad, she was shocked to find that the vibrant underwater world she had once known was disappearing before her eyes.

Rising sea temperatures and ocean acidification had taken their toll on the delicate coral reefs that fringed the coastline, bleaching them bone white and leaving behind a barren underwater wasteland. The once-thriving ecosystem teeming with life had been reduced to a ghostly shadow of its former self.

Determined to uncover the truth behind the devastation, Lila dove into her research with renewed vigor. She spent her days diving beneath the waves, documenting the changes in the marine environment and studying the impact of climate change on the local marine life. But the more she learned, the more her heart ached for the world she had lost.

One evening, as the sun dipped below the horizon and painted the sky in shades of pink and gold, Lila sat alone on the beach, her thoughts consumed by despair. How could she stand idly by and watch as her beloved ocean suffered? What could one person do in the face of such overwhelming destruction?

Lost in her thoughts, Lila didn't notice the figure approaching until he was standing beside her, his weathered face etched with lines of wisdom and kindness. It was Old Man Wilson, a retired fisherman who had spent his entire life on the sea.

"Troubled waters, eh?" he said, his voice gruff but gentle.

Lila nodded, unable to find the words to express the heaviness in her heart.

Old Man Wilson settled himself beside her, his eyes fixed on the horizon where the last rays of sunlight danced on the water.

"I've seen a lot of changes in these waters over the years," he said, his voice tinged with sadness. "But I've also seen the resilience of the ocean, how it has the power to heal itself if given the chance."

Lila turned to him, a glimmer of hope flickering in her eyes. "Do you really think so?"

Old Man Wilson nodded, a faint smile tugging at the corners of his lips. "I do. But it'll take more than just hope to make a difference. It'll take action. And sometimes, all it takes is one person to start a ripple that can turn into a wave of change."

As Lila listened to his words, a spark ignited within her. Perhaps she couldn't single-handedly save the ocean, but she could be the catalyst for change in her community. She could inspire others to care for the ocean as deeply as she did, to take action to protect it for future generations.

With renewed determination, Lila rose to her feet, her heart brimming with purpose. She would be the seed of hope that Seaview Cove so desperately needed, the spark that would ignite a movement to heal the ocean and restore its beauty for all to enjoy.

And as she looked out at the vast expanse of sea stretching out before her, she knew that no matter how daunting the task ahead, she would face it with courage, passion, and a steadfast belief in the power of one person to make a difference.

For in the heart of every wave, in the depths of every ocean, there lay a seed of hope, waiting to be nurtured and cultivated into something beautiful and enduring. And Lila was determined to be the one to plant it.

# Part 2: The Ripple Effect

As the days turned into weeks, Lila threw herself into her mission with unwavering determination. She organized beach clean-up events, rallying the residents of Seaview Cove to join her in removing litter and debris from the shores. Together, they filled countless bags with trash, clearing the beaches of plastic bottles, discarded fishing nets, and other pollutants that threatened the health of the ocean.

But Lila knew that cleaning up the beaches was only the first step. To truly make a difference, she needed to inspire a deeper connection to the ocean and foster a sense of stewardship among the community.

With this goal in mind, Lila teamed up with local schools to develop educational programs focused on marine conservation. She visited classrooms, sharing her knowledge and passion for the ocean with students of all ages. Together, they learned about the importance of preserving marine habitats, protecting endangered species, and reducing their carbon footprint to mitigate the effects of climate change.

The response from the community was overwhelmingly positive, and soon, Lila found herself surrounded by a dedicated group of volunteers eager to join her cause. Together, they formed the Seaview Cove Ocean Conservation Society, a grassroots organization committed to protecting the ocean and promoting sustainability in their community.

Under Lila's leadership, the society launched a series of initiatives aimed at reducing plastic waste, promoting responsible fishing practices, and advocating for the creation of marine protected areas along the coastline.

They worked tirelessly to raise awareness about the importance of preserving the ocean and inspired others to take action to protect it.

As word of their efforts spread, support for the cause grew, and soon, the ripple of change that Lila had started began to spread far beyond the shores of Seaview Cove. Other coastal communities took notice of their success and began implementing similar conservation measures, creating a ripple effect that stretched along the coastline and beyond.

But Lila knew that their work was far from over. Climate change continued to pose a threat to the ocean, and the challenges they faced were daunting. Yet, she remained undeterred, fueled by the knowledge that every small action had the power to make a difference.

As she stood on the beach, watching the waves crash against the shore, Lila felt a sense of pride swell within her. Though the road ahead was long and uncertain, she knew that as long as she and her fellow ocean guardians remained steadfast in their commitment to protecting the ocean, there was hope for a brighter future.

And so, with the support of her community by her side, Lila continued to fight for the ocean she loved, knowing that together, they could create a ripple of change that would

echo across the seas for generations

to come.

# <u>Part 3 : A Beacon of Hope</u>

As the Seaview Cove Ocean Conservation Society's efforts gained momentum, Lila and her fellow ocean guardians found themselves at the forefront of a growing movement to protect the ocean and combat climate change. Their small coastal town had become a beacon of hope, inspiring communities near and far to take action to preserve the planet's precious resources.

With each passing day, Lila witnessed the ripple effect of their actions spreading across the globe. From remote island nations threatened by rising sea levels to bustling metropolises grappling with pollution, people everywhere were rising up to demand change and fight for a sustainable future.

But amidst the progress and victories, Lila couldn't shake the nagging sense of urgency that gnawed at her conscience. Despite their best efforts, the ocean continued to suffer, its fragile ecosystems pushed to the brink of collapse by the relentless march of climate change.

Determined to do more, Lila and her colleagues embarked on a bold new initiative to address the root causes of environmental degradation and promote systemic change on a global scale. They partnered with international organizations, lobbied policymakers, and mobilized grassroots activists to push for ambitious climate action and environmental policies.

Their efforts bore fruit, as governments around the world began to take meaningful steps to address climate change and protect the planet's natural resources. From implementing renewable energy initiatives to enacting stricter regulations on carbon emissions, the world was slowly but surely moving towards a more sustainable future.

But the fight was far from over. Climate change remained an existential threat, and the consequences of inaction were becoming increasingly dire. As extreme weather events intensified and ecosystems collapsed, Lila knew that they couldn't afford to rest on their laurels.

With renewed determination, she redoubled her efforts to raise awareness about the urgency of the climate crisis and inspire others to join the fight for a sustainable future. She traveled the world, speaking at conferences and events, sharing her experiences and insights, and mobilizing people from all walks of life to take action.

And slowly, but surely, the tide began to turn. The voices of the people grew louder, the calls for change more insistent. Governments and corporations alike were forced to listen, as the groundswell of public pressure demanded bold and decisive action to address the climate crisis.

As Lila stood on the beach, watching the sun sink below the horizon, she felt a sense of hope swell within her. Though the road ahead would be long and challenging, she knew that as long as people like her continued to fight for the planet they loved, there was hope for a brighter future.

And so, with the wind at her back and the ocean at her side, Lila continued to march forward, a beacon of hope in a world threatened by darkness. For in her heart, she knew that the power to create change lay within each and every one of us, waiting to be unleashed and harnessed for the greater good of all.

# Part 4 : Embracing Unity

As Lila's efforts to combat climate change and protect the ocean gained momentum, she found herself at the center of a growing movement of activists, scientists, and concerned citizens united in their mission to safeguard the planet for future generations.

Together, they worked tirelessly to raise awareness about the urgent need for climate action and advocate for policies that would mitigate the effects of climate change and protect vulnerable ecosystems.

In boardrooms and conference halls, they engaged with policymakers and industry leaders, urging them to prioritize sustainability and invest in renewable energy and green technologies. They called for bold and decisive action to reduce carbon emissions and transition to a low-carbon economy, recognizing that the window of opportunity to avert catastrophic climate change was rapidly closing.

But their work went beyond mere advocacy and lobbying. They also sought to inspire individual action and empower communities to take ownership of their environmental future.

Through educational programs and grassroots initiatives, they encouraged people from all walks of life to adopt more sustainable lifestyles and reduce their ecological footprint. They promoted conservation efforts and restoration projects, empowering local communities to protect and restore their natural environments.

One such project was the creation of community-led conservation areas, where residents worked together to preserve and protect their local ecosystems. From reforestation efforts to the establishment of marine protected areas, these initiatives empowered communities to take control of their environmental destiny and ensure the long-term health and vitality of their surroundings.

As the movement grew, so too did the sense of unity and solidarity among its members. People from all corners of the globe came together, united by a shared sense of purpose and a common commitment to protecting the planet they called home.

In the face of daunting challenges and seemingly insurmountable odds, they found strength in their collective efforts and the knowledge that they were not alone in their fight. Together, they forged a path forward, guided by their shared values of compassion, stewardship, and a deep reverence for the natural world.

And as they looked towards the future, they did so with hope and determination, knowing that their collective action had the power to shape a better world for themselves, their children, and all living beings that called planet Earth home.

# Part 5 The Power of Collaboration

As the movement to combat climate change and protect the environment gained momentum, Lila and her fellow activists recognized the power of collaboration in driving meaningful change. They understood that no single individual or organization could solve the complex challenges facing the planet alone – it would require a united effort from people and communities around the world.

With this in mind, Lila and her colleagues worked tirelessly to build bridges between different sectors and stakeholders, fostering partnerships and alliances that transcended geographic, cultural, and political boundaries.

They reached out to businesses and corporations, urging them to adopt more sustainable practices and invest in renewable energy and green technologies. They collaborated with academic institutions and research organizations, leveraging scientific expertise to inform policy decisions and drive innovation.

They also engaged with grassroots movements and community organizations, empowering local communities to take ownership of their environmental future and advocate for change at the grassroots level.

Through these collaborative efforts, they were able to amplify their impact and effect meaningful change on a global scale. From implementing renewable energy projects in developing countries to launching initiatives to protect biodiversity hotspots, their collective action had a tangible and lasting impact on the planet and its inhabitants.

But perhaps the most powerful aspect of their collaboration was the sense of solidarity and camaraderie it fostered among those involved. People from diverse backgrounds and perspectives came together, united by a common goal and a shared sense of purpose.

They learned from one another, drawing inspiration and strength from the stories and experiences of their fellow activists. They celebrated each other's successes and supported one another in times of difficulty, recognizing that they were all part of a larger movement working towards a common goal.

And as they worked together to address the urgent challenges of climate change and environmental degradation, they found hope and resilience in their collective efforts. They knew that by standing together and supporting one another, they could overcome any obstacle and create a better, more sustainable future for all.

In the end, it was this spirit of collaboration and solidarity that drove meaningful change and paved the way for a brighter future for the planet and its inhabitants. And as Lila looked towards the horizon, she knew that their work was far from over – but with their collective efforts, they had laid the foundation for a more sustainable

and equitable world for generations to
come.

# Part 6 The Ripple Effect



As Lila and her fellow activists continued their efforts to combat climate change and protect the environment, they began to witness the ripple effect of their actions spreading far and wide, touching the lives of people and communities around the world.

Their advocacy and activism had inspired others to take action in their own communities, sparking a wave of grassroots movements and initiatives aimed at addressing environmental issues and promoting sustainability.

In cities and towns across the globe, people came together to plant trees, clean up beaches, and advocate for stronger environmental policies. They organized marches and protests, demanding action from their governments and holding corporations accountable for their environmental impact.

These grassroots movements gained momentum, capturing the attention of policymakers and industry leaders and driving meaningful change at the local, national, and international levels.

Governments began to implement policies to reduce carbon emissions, protect natural habitats, and invest in renewable energy. Corporations adopted more sustainable practices, committing to reduce their carbon footprint and minimize their environmental impact.

The ripple effect of these actions extended beyond environmental conservation, leading to broader social and economic changes. Communities became more resilient and self-sufficient, investing in renewable energy infrastructure and sustainable agriculture practices.

People became more aware of their impact on the planet and took steps to live more sustainably, reducing their consumption, conserving resources, and adopting eco-friendly habits.

The ripple effect of Lila's activism and the efforts of countless others like her had transformed the world, paving the way for a more sustainable and equitable future for all.

As Lila looked out at the world she had helped to shape, she felt a deep sense of pride and gratitude. Though the challenges of climate change and environmental degradation were far from over, she knew that the ripple effect of their actions would continue to spread, inspiring change and driving progress for generations to come.


And as she stood on the beach, watching the waves crash against the shore, she felt a renewed sense of hope and determination. For in the end, she knew that the power to create change lay within each and every one of us – and that together, we could build a better world for ourselves and for future generations.

# Part 7 The Turning Tide



As the tide of public opinion began to turn, governments and corporations alike were forced to confront the realities of climate change and take meaningful action to address its devastating effects. From implementing renewable energy initiatives to enacting stricter regulations on carbon emissions, the world was slowly but surely moving towards a more sustainable future.

But the fight was far from over. Climate change remained an existential threat, and the consequences of inaction were becoming increasingly dire. Extreme weather events intensified, ecosystems collapsed, and communities around the world struggled to adapt to the rapidly changing climate.

In the face of these challenges, Lila and her fellow activists redoubled their efforts to raise awareness about the urgency of the climate crisis and advocate for bold and decisive action to address its root causes. They organized rallies and protests, lobbied policymakers, and mobilized grassroots movements to demand change at all levels of society.

Their efforts were met with resistance from powerful vested interests determined to maintain the status quo. But Lila and her colleagues refused to back down, drawing strength from their shared commitment to protecting the planet and its inhabitants.

They knew that the road ahead would be long and challenging, but they remained undeterred in their determination to create a better, more sustainable world for future generations.

And as they looked towards the horizon, they did so with hope and determination, knowing that the power to create change lay within each and every one of us – and that together, we could build a brighter future for ourselves and for all living beings that called planet Earth home.

# Part 8 A Global Awakening

As Lila and her fellow activists continued to raise awareness about the urgency of the climate crisis, they began to witness a groundswell of support from people and communities around the world. From small towns to bustling cities, people of all ages and backgrounds were coming together to demand action on climate change and environmental issues.

The youth-led climate strikes inspired by activists like Greta Thunberg grew into a global movement, with millions of young people taking to the streets to demand meaningful action from their governments. Their impassioned pleas for climate justice resonated with people of all ages, sparking a wave of activism and solidarity that crossed borders and continents.

Governments and corporations were forced to take notice, as public pressure mounted and the urgency of the climate crisis became impossible to ignore. Leaders from around the world gathered at international summits to negotiate agreements aimed at reducing carbon emissions and limiting global warming to manageable levels.

Investment in renewable energy and green technologies soared, as governments and businesses alike recognized the economic and environmental benefits of transitioning to a low-carbon economy. From solar panels to wind turbines, clean energy infrastructure began to replace outdated fossil fuel-based systems, paving the way for a more sustainable future.

But perhaps the most significant change was the shift in public consciousness that accompanied this global awakening. People everywhere began to reevaluate their relationship with the planet and take steps to live more sustainably, reducing their consumption, conserving resources, and adopting eco-friendly habits.

The collective action of individuals and communities around the world sent a powerful message to policymakers and industry leaders: the time for action on climate change was now, and the stakes could not be higher.

As Lila looked out at the world she had helped to shape, she felt a profound sense of gratitude and hope. Though the challenges of climate change and environmental degradation were far from over, she knew that the global awakening she had witnessed was a testament to the power of collective action and the resilience of the human spirit.

And as she stood on the beach, watching the waves crash against the shore, she felt a renewed sense of optimism for the future. For in the end, she knew that the power to create change lay within each and every one of us – and that together, we could build a better world for ourselves and for future generations.

# Part 9 The Path Forward

As the world grappled with the urgent challenges of climate change and environmental degradation, Lila and her fellow activists continued to push for bold and decisive action to address the root causes of these crises.

They worked tirelessly to raise awareness about the interconnected nature of environmental issues and the urgent need for systemic change.

They engaged with policymakers,

industry leaders, and grassroots

organizations to develop and

implement solutions that would

protect the planet and its inhabitants

for generations to come.


From advocating for stronger

environmental regulations to

promoting renewable energy

initiatives, their efforts were aimed at

creating a more sustainable and equitable world for all.

But the road ahead was fraught with challenges, and the work was far from over. Climate change continued to pose an existential threat, and the consequences of inaction were becoming increasingly dire.

Extreme weather events intensified, ecosystems collapsed, and vulnerable communities around the world bore the brunt of the impacts. The need for action was urgent, and the stakes could not be higher.

Yet amidst the challenges and uncertainties, Lila remained steadfast in her commitment to creating a better world. She drew strength from the collective action of individuals and communities around the world, knowing that together, they could overcome any obstacle and build a brighter future for themselves and for future generations.

And as she looked towards the horizon, she did so with hope and determination, knowing that the path forward would be difficult but that the power to create change lay within each and every one of us.

For in the end, she knew that the fate of the planet rested in our hands – and that together, we could forge a path towards a more sustainable, equitable, and resilient world for all.

# **<u>Part 10 A New Dawn</u>**

As the sun rose on a new day, casting its golden light across the land, Lila felt a sense of optimism and hope wash over her. The challenges of climate change and environmental degradation remained daunting, but she knew that they were not insurmountable.

For in the face of adversity, she had witnessed the power of collective action and the resilience of the human spirit. She had seen communities come together to protect the planet and its inhabitants, and she had felt the groundswell of support from people of all ages and backgrounds who were committed to creating a better world.

And as she looked towards the future, she did so with a renewed sense of purpose and determination. For she knew that the path forward would be difficult, but that together, we could overcome any obstacle and build a brighter, more sustainable future for ourselves and for future generations.

For in the end, she believed that the power to create change lay within each and every one of us – and that together, we could forge a new dawn for the planet and all who call it home.

And so, with hope in her heart and a steadfast commitment to the cause, Lila embarked on the next chapter of her journey, ready to continue the fight for a better world – a world where the beauty of nature is cherished, the planet is protected, and all living beings can thrive in harmony with the earth.

And as she took her first steps towards this brighter future, she knew that the journey would be long and challenging, but that with the power of unity, determination, and love for the planet, anything was possible.

For in the end, she believed that together, we could change the world.

# <u>Reader Feedback and Reviews</u>

Thank you for reading "Echoes of Earth: Stories of Resilience and Renewal in the Face of Climate Change." Your feedback is invaluable to us and helps shape future works.

**I'd Love to Hear From You** Please share your thoughts, insights, and suggestions by contacting me at:

**Email:** nadirhazarika@gmail.com

**Leave a Review** If you enjoyed this collection, please consider leaving a review on **Amazon**. Your reviews help other readers discover our stories and support our mission to spread awareness about climate resilience and renewal.

Thank you for your support and for being part of our community!

Warm regards,
Nadir Hussain Hazarika